The Gospel of
MARK

Introduction by
Fr Javier Ruiz-Ortiz

Larger Print Edition

*All booklets are published
thanks to the generosity of the supporters
of the Catholic Truth Society*

ESV

The *English Standard Version*, ESV, and the ESV logo are registered trademarks of Good News Publishers. *English Standard Version*, ESV, and the ESV logo are registered in the United States of America. ESV and the ESV logo are registered in the United Kingdom and the European Union. Used by permission.

The Gospel text is from the *English Standard Version of the Bible, Catholic Edition* (ESV-CE), published by Asian Trading Corporation, © 2017 by Crossway. All rights are reserved. *The English Standard Version of the Bible, Catholic Edition* is published in the United Kingdom by SPCK Publishing.

First published © 2024 The Incorporated Catholic Truth Society, 42-46 Harleyford Road, London SE11 5AY. Tel: 020 7640 0042. www.ctsbooks.org

ISBN 978 1 78469 813 3

Introduction to the Gospel of
MARK

Gospel

"The beginning of the gospel of Jesus Christ, the Son of God" (1:1)

The second book of the New Testament begins with these words, which should be the lens through which the whole work is to be read. The story of Jesus is given to us in four different outlines (according to Matthew, Mark, Luke and John) under the common name of gospel.

First and foremost, "gospel" (*euangelium,*) refers, in the ancient world, to the proclamation of the victories and deeds of an emperor whereas in the Old Testament the term refers to the action of God liberating the people of Israel from Exile (*Isa* 40:9). In the New Testament the term is referred to the mission of Jesus: "to proclaim good news to the poor" (*Luke* 4:18), a good news which is summarised by Mark as "the time is fulfilled, and the kingdom of God is at hand; repent and believe the gospel." (1:15). Gospel, then refers to the preaching of the good news or *kerygma*, namely, the proclamation of the saving events in the life of Christ (the passion, death, resurrection and ascension into heaven of Christ) which changed the lives of people and communities. This proclamation was done as part of the missionary outburst of the church, an announcement which subsequently modelled the Christian community.

As we see, Jesus is both the object and the subject of the proclamation. The concept of gospel takes us back to the oral tradition and preaching of the saving events, which precedes the recording of those events. Then, in a second sense, the term gospel applies to the written document. This document is not a biography in the narrow sense but, while the orderly account of true events takes a prominent part of the composition, a true theology is also developed. The gospel of Mark needs to be put in its relationship with Matthew and Luke. Together they are called the "synoptic" gospels because they share a similar structure and sequence of events culminating in the passion, death and resurrection of Jesus. One could put the three gospels side by side and look at them with one view (*syn* – with; *optic* – view/glance).

Mark was recognised as the author of this gospel from ancient times, even though there is no attribution to him in the text. He is identified with one of Paul's companions (*Acts* 13;13; 15:37-39; *Col* 4:10-11; *2 Tim* 4:9-11) who at some point would have followed Peter and settled with him in Rome where he wrote the gospel. There is no direct mention of the Fall of Jerusalem in AD 70 hence it was probably composed before that event. It seems to be addressed to pagans as there are not many references to Scripture, the Hebrew and Aramaic terms are translated and Jewish customs are explained. Some of the beneficiaries of Jesus' ministry are pagans, who show a degree of faith superior to that of the Jewish characters

INTRODUCTION

(5:1-20; 7:24-30). The addressees must be going through a time of external turmoil and persecution which is reflected in the way the story is told and emphasis on the need to undergo persecutions (cf. *Mark* 10:30). Scholars have identified the period of Caligula or Nero as the historical background to what is recounted by the gospel. Hence the composition would have taken place in the 60's or early 70's in Rome.

Who is Jesus?

Mark organises his gospel in four parts: a prologue (1:1-13); a part dominated by the question on the identity of Jesus (1:14 – 8:30); a part explaining what discipleship means (8:31 – 14:50) and a section dedicated to the Paschal Mystery (14:51 – 16:20). In all of them he shows who is "Jesus Christ, the Son of God". From the point of view of the reader, we know that the manifestation of Jesus as the Christ, the Son of God is at stake at every stage of the journey and all events, even the most unfortunate, are geared towards that end. In this way we know more than the characters, who little by little discover the identity of Jesus. In most of the accounts, not everyone recognises him for who he is; however, there are a few characters who discover who he is at transcendental moments, such as Peter at the end of the second section or the centurion at the end of the third section. Half way through the narrative, when Jesus asks the disciples: "But who do you say that

I am?" Peter answers him, "You are the Christ." (*Mark* 8:29). Further, after the crucifixion, a pagan makes the ultimate profession of faith: "And when the centurion, who stood facing Jesus, saw that in this way he breathed his last, he said, "Truly this man was the Son of God!" (*Mark* 15:39). This expression of belief is set in contrast with the refusal to accept Jesus expressed by the High Priest during the religious process against Jesus (cf. 14:61-64).

Otherwise, the question all through the gospel account is "who is Jesus?" Straight after Peter's profession of faith, we find the account of the Transfiguration (*Mark* 9:2-13). Those who are present see Jesus in his glory and are ordered not to tell anyone what they have seen (9:9). Jesus, even though he performs miracles openly (2:1-12; 3:1-5), seems to hide his identity from the public and even, when he exercises his authority over illness or the powers of evil, he is clear that those who benefit from his extraordinary power are to say nothing (1:25, 44). This silence imposed in the narration allows a dialogue between the reader and the text. The reader is invited to reflect on what has been expressed, both reflecting on the identity of Jesus and the way his follower is called to behave. For example, when Jesus orders the storm to calm down, the disciples wonder: "Who then is this, that even the wind and the sea obey him?" (*Mark* 4:41). This question then is posed to those who read the story and expects an answer.

INTRODUCTION

The Disciples' response

The disciples, therefore, not only stand in awe and wonder at the actions of the master, but they do not understand his teaching. When on three occasion he reveals what his mission is, namely, to go to Jerusalem in order to suffer, die and rise again (8:31; 9:30; 10:32), they want the opposite (9:34; 10:36). Again and again the gospel explains that following Jesus means that the disciple should "take his cross and follow him" (cf. 8:34). Those who follow Jesus need to give up everything, even their own ideas (cf. 8:35; 12:41-44; 14:3). This is expressed in different ways in the narration, for example the idea of leaving behind one's covering and security like the blind man Bartimeus and following Jesus along the way (10:50-52). This allegory has as its ultimate expression the image of the young man who leaves all his clothes at the beginning of the passion (cf. 14:51-52).

Jesus meets people in different places which should also be interpreted in light of his revelation as the Christ, the Son of God. He visits the synagogue (1:21; 3:1; 6:2), goes into people's houses (1:29; 5:38; 7:3) or boards a boat (4:1; 4:36; 6:51). As well as the private dwellings, Jesus is also seen in public places (6:53; 7:33), as he makes his way to Jerusalem. Some of his most powerful teachings and actions are done at table where he shares his life with those present at that time (2:15; 7:1-2). One should also think of the two occasions in which he multiplies the loaves and fish (6:35-44; 8:1-9) which are described with the same verbs as the Last Supper (14:17-25): "to take", "to bless", "to break" and "to give". Thus, Mark points to the passion throughout the gospel.

Jerusalem

Jesus' journey has Jerusalem as its final destination. It is at the city that Jesus accomplished his Paschal Mystery (passion, death and resurrection). Within this context Jesus gives a long discourse about the end of times (13:1-37) and meets the different groups who have been hostile from the beginning of the account (12:1-34; cf. 3:6). It is at the end of an account of atrocious suffering that Jesus is acknowledged as Son of God (15:39), an affirmation that can only be understood through the prism of the cross. Similarly, the one who wants to follow Jesus is called to "deny himself and take his cross and follow him" (cf. 8:34). Thus, some have explained that the gospel was written with those who wanted to join the Christian community in mind, giving them a model of what following Jesus means, and also giving the first disciples as an example of the communion Jesus develops with his followers (1:16-20; 16:7).

Conclusion

As one begins to read the gospel of Mark, one should have at the back of one's mind the opening verse and wonder how any specific passage presents Jesus as the Christ, the Son of God.

THE GOSPEL ACCORDING TO
MARK

John the Baptist Prepares the Way

1 The beginning of the gospel of Jesus Christ, the Son of God.[a]
2 As it is written in Isaiah the prophet,[b]

"Behold, I send my messenger before your face,
  who will prepare your way,
3 the voice of one crying in the wilderness:
  'Prepare[c] the way of the Lord,
  make his paths straight,'"

4 John appeared, baptizing in the wilderness and proclaiming a baptism of repentance for the forgiveness of sins. 5 And all the country of Judea and all Jerusalem were going out to him and were being baptized by him in the river Jordan, confessing their sins. 6 Now John was clothed with camel's hair and wore a leather belt round his waist and ate locusts and wild honey. 7 And he preached, saying, "After me comes he who is mightier than I, the strap of whose sandals I am not worthy to stoop down and untie. 8 I have baptized you with water, but he will baptize you with the Holy Spirit."

1a Some manuscripts omit *the Son of God*
1b Some manuscripts *in the prophets*
1c Or *crying: Prepare in the wilderness*

The Baptism of Jesus

⁹ In those days Jesus came from Nazareth of Galilee and was baptized by John in the Jordan. ¹⁰ And when he came up out of the water, immediately he saw the heavens being torn open and the Spirit descending on him like a dove. ¹¹ And a voice came from heaven, "You are my beloved Son;[d] with you I am well pleased."

The Temptation of Jesus

¹² The Spirit immediately drove him out into the wilderness. ¹³ And he was in the wilderness forty days, being tempted by Satan. And he was with the wild animals, and the angels were ministering to him.

Jesus Begins His Ministry

¹⁴ Now after John was arrested, Jesus came into Galilee, proclaiming the gospel of God, ¹⁵ and saying, "The time is fulfilled, and the kingdom of God is at hand;[e] repent and believe in the gospel."

Jesus Calls the First Disciples

¹⁶ Passing alongside the Sea of Galilee, he saw Simon and Andrew the brother of Simon casting a net into the sea, for they were fishermen. ¹⁷ And Jesus said to them,

---

[1d.] Or *my Son, my* (or *the*) *Beloved*
[1e.] Or *the kingdom of God has come near*

"Follow me, and I will make you become fishers of men."*f*
¹⁸ And immediately they left their nets and followed him. ¹⁹ And going on a little farther, he saw James the son of Zebedee and John his brother, who were in their boat mending the nets. ²⁰ And immediately he called them, and they left their father Zebedee in the boat with the hired servants and followed him.

Jesus Heals a Man with an Unclean Spirit

²¹ And they went into Capernaum, and immediately on the Sabbath he entered the synagogue and was teaching. ²² And they were astonished at his teaching, for he taught them as one who had authority, and not as the scribes. ²³ And immediately there was in their synagogue a man with an unclean spirit. And he cried out, ²⁴ "What have you to do with us, Jesus of Nazareth? Have you come to destroy us? I know who you are – the Holy One of God." ²⁵ But Jesus rebuked him, saying, "Be silent, and come out of him!" ²⁶ And the unclean spirit, convulsing him and crying out with a loud voice, came out of him. ²⁷ And they were all amazed, so that they questioned among themselves, saying, "What is this? A new teaching with authority! He commands even the unclean spirits, and they obey him." ²⁸ And at once his fame spread everywhere throughout all the surrounding region of Galilee.

1f. The Greek word *anthropoi* refers here to both men and women

Jesus Heals Many

²⁹ And immediately he[g] left the synagogue and entered the house of Simon and Andrew, with James and John. ³⁰ Now Simon's mother-in-law lay ill with a fever, and immediately they told him about her. ³¹ And he came and took her by the hand and lifted her up, and the fever left her, and she began to serve them.

³² That evening at sunset they brought to him all who were sick or oppressed by demons. ³³ And the whole city was gathered together at the door. ³⁴ And he healed many who were sick with various diseases, and cast out many demons. And he would not permit the demons to speak, because they knew him.

Jesus Preaches in Galilee

³⁵ And rising very early in the morning, while it was still dark, he departed and went out to a desolate place, and there he prayed. ³⁶ And Simon and those who were with him searched for him, ³⁷ and they found him and said to him, "Everyone is looking for you." ³⁸ And he said to them, "Let us go on to the next towns, that I may preach there also, for that is what I came for." ³⁹ And he went throughout all Galilee, preaching in their synagogues and casting out demons.

---

[g] Some manuscripts *they*

Jesus Cleanses a Leper

⁴⁰ And a leper[h] came to him, imploring him, and kneeling said to him, "If you will, you can make me clean." ⁴¹ Moved with pity, he stretched out his hand and touched him and said to him, "I will; be clean." ⁴² And immediately the leprosy left him, and he was made clean. ⁴³ And Jesus[i] sternly charged him and sent him away at once, ⁴⁴ and said to him, "See that you say nothing to anyone, but go, show yourself to the priest and offer for your cleansing what Moses commanded, for a proof to them." ⁴⁵ But he went out and began to talk freely about it, and to spread the news, so that Jesus could no longer openly enter a town, but was out in desolate places, and people were coming to him from every quarter.

Jesus Heals a Paralytic

2 And when he returned to Capernaum after some days, it was reported that he was at home. ² And many were gathered together, so that there was no more room, not even at the door. And he was preaching the word to them. ³ And they came, bringing to him a paralytic carried by four men. ⁴ And when they could not get near him because of the crowd, they removed the roof above him, and when they had made an opening, they let down

---

[1h]. *Leprosy* was a term for several skin diseases; see Leviticus 13
[1i]. Greek *he*; also verse 45

the bed on which the paralytic lay. ⁵ And when Jesus saw their faith, he said to the paralytic, "Son, your sins are forgiven." ⁶ Now some of the scribes were sitting there, questioning in their hearts, ⁷ "Why does this man speak like that? He is blaspheming! Who can forgive sins but God alone?" ⁸ And immediately Jesus, perceiving in his spirit that they thus questioned within themselves, said to them, "Why do you question these things in your hearts? ⁹ Which is easier, to say to the paralytic, 'Your sins are forgiven', or to say, 'Rise, take up your bed and walk'? ¹⁰ But that you may know that the Son of Man has authority on earth to forgive sins" – he said to the paralytic – ¹¹ "I say to you, rise, pick up your bed, and go home." ¹² And he rose and immediately picked up his bed and went out before them all, so that they were all amazed and glorified God, saying, "We never saw anything like this!"

Jesus Calls Levi

¹³ He went out again beside the lake, and all the crowd was coming to him, and he was teaching them. ¹⁴ And as he passed by, he saw Levi the son of Alphaeus sitting at the tax booth, and he said to him, "Follow me." And he rose and followed him.

¹⁵ And as he reclined at table in his house, many tax collectors and sinners were reclining with Jesus and his disciples, for there were many who followed him.

¹⁶ And the scribes of*ᵃ* the Pharisees, when they saw that he was eating with sinners and tax collectors, said to his disciples, "Why does he eat*ᵇ* with tax collectors and sinners?" ¹⁷ And when Jesus heard it, he said to them, "Those who are well have no need of a physician, but those who are sick. I came not to call the righteous, but sinners."

A Question About Fasting

¹⁸ Now John's disciples and the Pharisees were fasting. And people came and said to him, "Why do John's disciples and the disciples of the Pharisees fast, but your disciples do not fast?" ¹⁹ And Jesus said to them, "Can the wedding guests fast while the bridegroom is with them? As long as they have the bridegroom with them, they cannot fast. ²⁰ The days will come when the bridegroom is taken away from them, and then they will fast in that day. ²¹ No one sews a piece of unshrunk cloth on an old garment. If he does, the patch tears away from it, the new from the old, and a worse tear is made. ²² And no one puts new wine into old wineskins. If he does, the wine will burst the skins – and the wine is destroyed, and so are the skins. But new wine is for fresh wineskins."*ᶜ*

2a. Some manuscripts *and*
2b. Some manuscripts add *and drink*
2c. Some manuscripts omit *But new wine is for fresh wineskins*

Jesus Is Lord of the Sabbath

²³ One Sabbath he was going through the cornfields, and as they made their way, his disciples began to pluck ears of corn. ²⁴ And the Pharisees were saying to him, "Look, why are they doing what is not lawful on the Sabbath?" ²⁵ And he said to them, "Have you never read what David did, when he was in need and was hungry, he and those who were with him: ²⁶ how he entered the house of God, in the time of*ᵈ* Abiathar the high priest, and ate the bread of the Presence, which it is not lawful for any but the priests to eat, and also gave it to those who were with him?" ²⁷ And he said to them, "The Sabbath was made for man, not man for the Sabbath. ²⁸ So the Son of Man is lord even of the Sabbath."

A Man with a Withered Hand

3 Again he entered the synagogue, and a man was there with a withered hand. ² And they watched Jesus,*ᵃ* to see whether he would heal him on the Sabbath, so that they might accuse him. ³ And he said to the man with the withered hand, "Come here." ⁴ And he said to them, "Is it lawful on the Sabbath to do good or to do harm, to save life or to kill?" But they were silent. ⁵ And he looked round at them with anger, grieved at their hardness of heart, and said to the man, "Stretch out your

---

2d. Or *in the passage about*
3a. Greek *him*

hand." He stretched it out, and his hand was restored. ⁶ The Pharisees went out and immediately held counsel with the Herodians against him, how to destroy him.

A Great Crowd Follows Jesus

⁷ Jesus withdrew with his disciples to the sea, and a great crowd followed, from Galilee and Judea ⁸ and Jerusalem and Idumea and from beyond the Jordan and from around Tyre and Sidon. When the great crowd heard all that he was doing, they came to him. ⁹ And he told his disciples to have a boat ready for him because of the crowd, lest they crush him, ¹⁰ for he had healed many, so that all who had diseases pressed around him to touch him. ¹¹ And whenever the unclean spirits saw him, they fell down before him and cried out, "You are the Son of God." ¹² And he strictly ordered them not to make him known.

The Twelve Apostles

¹³ And he went up on the mountain and called to him those whom he desired, and they came to him. ¹⁴ And he appointed twelve (whom he also named apostles) so that they might be with him and he might send them out to preach ¹⁵ and have authority to cast out demons. ¹⁶ He appointed the twelve: Simon (to whom he gave the name Peter); ¹⁷ James the son of Zebedee and John the brother of James (to whom he gave the name Boanerges, that is, Sons of Thunder); ¹⁸ Andrew, and Philip, and Bartholomew, and Matthew, and Thomas, and James the

son of Alphaeus, and Thaddaeus, and Simon the Zealot,[b] [19] and Judas Iscariot, who betrayed him.

[20] Then he went home, and the crowd gathered again, so that they could not even eat. [21] And when his family heard it, they went out to seize him, for they were saying, "He is out of his mind."

Blasphemy Against the Holy Spirit

[22] And the scribes who came down from Jerusalem were saying, "He is possessed by Beelzebul," and "by the prince of demons he casts out the demons." [23] And he called them to him and said to them in parables, "How can Satan cast out Satan? [24] If a kingdom is divided against itself, that kingdom cannot stand. [25] And if a house is divided against itself, that house will not be able to stand. [26] And if Satan has risen up against himself and is divided, he cannot stand, but is coming to an end. [27] But no one can enter a strong man's house and plunder his goods, unless he first binds the strong man. Then indeed he may plunder his house.

[28] "Truly, I say to you, all sins will be forgiven the children of man, and whatever blasphemies they utter, [29] but whoever blasphemes against the Holy Spirit never has forgiveness, but is guilty of an eternal sin" – [30] for they were saying, "He has an unclean spirit."

3b. Greek *kananaios*, meaning *zealot*

Jesus' Mother and Brothers

³¹ And his mother and his brothers came, and standing outside they sent to him and called him. ³² And a crowd was sitting around him, and they said to him, "Your mother and your brothers[c] are outside, seeking you." ³³ And he answered them, "Who are my mother and my brothers?" ³⁴ And looking about at those who sat around him, he said, "Here are my mother and my brothers! ³⁵ For whoever does the will of God, he is my brother and sister and mother."

The Parable of the Sower

4 Again he began to teach beside the sea. And a very large crowd gathered about him, so that he got into a boat and sat in it on the sea, and the whole crowd was beside the sea on the land. ² And he was teaching them many things in parables, and in his teaching he said to them: ³ "Listen! Behold, a sower went out to sow. ⁴ And as he sowed, some seed fell along the path, and the birds came and devoured it. ⁵ Other seed fell on rocky ground, where it did not have much soil, and immediately it sprang up, since it had no depth of soil. ⁶ And when the sun rose, it was scorched, and since it had no root, it withered away. ⁷ Other seed fell among thorns, and the thorns grew up and choked it, and it yielded no grain.

3c. Other manuscripts add *and your sisters*

⁸ And other seeds fell into good soil and produced grain, growing up and increasing and yielding thirtyfold and sixtyfold and a hundredfold." ⁹ And he said, "He who has ears to hear, let him hear."

The Purpose of the Parables

¹⁰ And when he was alone, those around him with the twelve asked him about the parables. ¹¹ And he said to them, "To you has been given the secret of the kingdom of God, but for those outside everything is in parables, ¹² so that

> "'they may indeed see but not perceive,
>   and may indeed hear but not understand,
>   lest they should turn and be forgiven.'"

¹³ And he said to them, "Do you not understand this parable? How then will you understand all the parables? ¹⁴ The sower sows the word. ¹⁵ And these are the ones along the path, where the word is sown: when they hear, Satan immediately comes and takes away the word that is sown in them. ¹⁶ And these are the ones sown on rocky ground: the ones who, when they hear the word, immediately receive it with joy. ¹⁷ And they have no root in themselves, but endure for a while; then, when tribulation or persecution arises on account of the word, immediately they fall away.[a] ¹⁸ And others are the ones

---

4a. Or *stumble*

sown among thorns. They are those who hear the word, [19] but the cares of the world and the deceitfulness of riches and the desires for other things enter in and choke the word, and it proves unfruitful. [20] But those that were sown on the good soil are the ones who hear the word and accept it and bear fruit, thirtyfold and sixtyfold and a hundredfold."

A Lamp Under a Basket

[21] And he said to them, "Is a lamp brought in to be put under a basket, or under a bed, and not on a stand? [22] For nothing is hidden except to be made manifest; nor is anything secret except to come to light. [23] If anyone has ears to hear, let him hear." [24] And he said to them, "Pay attention to what you hear: with the measure you use, it will be measured to you, and still more will be added to you. [25] For to the one who has, more will be given, and from the one who has not, even what he has will be taken away."

The Parable of the Seed Growing

[26] And he said, "The kingdom of God is as if a man should scatter seed on the ground. [27] He sleeps and rises night and day, and the seed sprouts and grows; he knows not how. [28] The earth produces by itself, first the blade, then the ear, then the full grain in the ear. [29] But when the grain is ripe, at once he puts in the sickle, because the harvest has come."

The Parable of the Mustard Seed

³⁰ And he said, "With what can we compare the kingdom of God, or what parable shall we use for it? ³¹ It is like a grain of mustard seed, which, when sown on the ground, is the smallest of all the seeds on earth, ³² yet when it is sown it grows up and becomes larger than all the garden plants and puts out large branches, so that the birds of the air can make nests in its shade."

³³ With many such parables he spoke the word to them, as they were able to hear it. ³⁴ He did not speak to them without a parable, but privately to his own disciples he explained everything.

Jesus Calms a Storm

³⁵ On that day, when evening had come, he said to them, "Let us go across to the other side." ³⁶ And leaving the crowd, they took him with them in the boat, just as he was. And other boats were with him. ³⁷ And a great windstorm arose, and the waves were breaking into the boat, so that the boat was already filling. ³⁸ But he was in the stern, asleep on the cushion. And they woke him and said to him, "Teacher, do you not care that we are perishing?" ³⁹ And he awoke and rebuked the wind and said to the sea, "Peace! Be still!" And the wind ceased, and there was a great calm. ⁴⁰ He said to them, "Why are you so afraid? Have you still no faith?" ⁴¹ And they were filled with great fear and said to one another, "Who then is this, that even the wind and the sea obey him?"

Jesus Heals a Man with a Demon

5 They came to the other side of the lake, to the country of the Gerasenes.[a] ² And when Jesus[b] had stepped out of the boat, immediately there met him out of the tombs a man with an unclean spirit. ³ He lived among the tombs. And no one could bind him any more, not even with a chain, ⁴ for he had often been bound with shackles and chains, but he wrenched the chains apart, and he broke the shackles in pieces. No one had the strength to subdue him. ⁵ Night and day among the tombs and on the mountains he was always crying out and cutting himself with stones. ⁶ And when he saw Jesus from afar, he ran and fell down before him. ⁷ And crying out with a loud voice, he said, "What have you to do with me, Jesus, Son of the Most High God? I adjure you by God, do not torment me." ⁸ For he was saying to him, "Come out of the man, you unclean spirit!" ⁹ And Jesus asked him, "What is your name?" He replied, "My name is Legion, for we are many." ¹⁰ And he begged him earnestly not to send them out of the country. ¹¹ Now a great herd of pigs was feeding there on the hillside, ¹² and they begged him, saying, "Send us to the pigs; let us enter them." ¹³ So he gave them permission. And the unclean spirits came out and entered the pigs; and the herd, numbering about

---

5a. Some manuscripts *Gergesenes*; some *Gadarenes*
5b. Greek *he*; also verse 9

two thousand, rushed down the steep bank into the sea and drowned in the sea.

¹⁴ The herdsmen fled and told it in the city and in the country. And people came to see what it was that had happened. ¹⁵ And they came to Jesus and saw the demon-possessed*c* man, the one who had had the legion, sitting there, clothed and in his right mind, and they were afraid. ¹⁶ And those who had seen it described to them what had happened to the demon-possessed man and to the pigs. ¹⁷ And they began to beg Jesus*d* to depart from their region. ¹⁸ As he was getting into the boat, the man who had been possessed with demons begged him that he might be with him. ¹⁹ And he did not permit him but said to him, "Go home to your friends and tell them how much the Lord has done for you, and how he has had mercy on you." ²⁰ And he went away and began to proclaim in the Decapolis how much Jesus had done for him, and everyone marvelled.

Jesus Heals a Woman and Jairus's Daughter

²¹ And when Jesus had crossed again in the boat to the other side, a great crowd gathered about him, and he was beside the sea. ²² Then came one of the rulers of

---

5c. Greek *daimonizomai* (demonized); also verses 16, 18; elsewhere rendered *oppressed by demons*
5d. Greek *him*

the synagogue, Jairus by name, and seeing him, he fell at his feet ²³ and implored him earnestly, saying, "My little daughter is at the point of death. Come and lay your hands on her, so that she may be made well and live." ²⁴ And he went with him.

And a great crowd followed him and thronged about him. ²⁵ And there was a woman who had had a discharge of blood for twelve years, ²⁶ and who had suffered much under many physicians, and had spent all that she had, and was no better but rather grew worse. ²⁷ She had heard the reports about Jesus and came up behind him in the crowd and touched his garment. ²⁸ For she said, "If I touch even his garments, I will be made well." ²⁹ And immediately the flow of blood dried up, and she felt in her body that she was healed of her disease. ³⁰ And Jesus, perceiving in himself that power had gone out from him, immediately turned about in the crowd and said, "Who touched my garments?" ³¹ And his disciples said to him, "You see the crowd pressing around you, and yet you say, 'Who touched me?'" ³² And he looked round to see who had done it. ³³ But the woman, knowing what had happened to her, came in fear and trembling and fell down before him and told him the whole truth. ³⁴ And he said to her, "Daughter, your faith has made you well; go in peace, and be healed of your disease."

³⁵ While he was still speaking, there came from the ruler's house some who said, "Your daughter is dead.

Why trouble the Teacher any further?" ³⁶ But overhearing[e] what they said, Jesus said to the ruler of the synagogue, "Do not fear, only believe." ³⁷ And he allowed no one to follow him except Peter and James and John the brother of James. ³⁸ They came to the house of the ruler of the synagogue, and Jesus[f] saw a commotion, people weeping and wailing loudly. ³⁹ And when he had entered, he said to them, "Why are you making a commotion and weeping? The child is not dead but sleeping." ⁴⁰ And they laughed at him. But he put them all outside and took the child's father and mother and those who were with him and went in where the child was. ⁴¹ Taking her by the hand he said to her, "Talitha cumi", which means, "Little girl, I say to you, arise." ⁴² And immediately the girl got up and began walking (for she was twelve years of age), and they were immediately overcome with amazement. ⁴³ And he strictly charged them that no one should know this, and told them to give her something to eat.

Jesus Rejected at Nazareth

6 He went away from there and came to his home town, and his disciples followed him. ² And on the Sabbath he began to teach in the synagogue, and many who heard him were astonished, saying, "Where did this man get these things? What is the wisdom given to him?

5e. Or *ignoring*; some manuscripts *hearing*
5f. Greek *he*

How are such mighty works done by his hands? ³ Is not this the carpenter, the son of Mary and brother of James and Joses and Judas and Simon? And are not his sisters here with us?" And they took offence at him. ⁴ And Jesus said to them, "A prophet is not without honour, except in his home town and among his relatives and in his own household." ⁵ And he could do no mighty work there, except that he laid his hands on a few sick people and healed them. ⁶ And he marvelled because of their unbelief.

And he went about among the villages teaching.

Jesus Sends Out the Twelve Apostles

⁷ And he called the twelve and began to send them out two by two, and gave them authority over the unclean spirits. ⁸ He charged them to take nothing for their journey except a staff – no bread, no bag, no money in their belts – ⁹ but to wear sandals and not put on two tunics.[a] ¹⁰ And he said to them, "Whenever you enter a house, stay there until you depart from there. ¹¹ And if any place will not receive you and they will not listen to you, when you leave, shake off the dust that is on your feet as a testimony against them." ¹² So they went out and proclaimed that people should repent. ¹³ And they cast out many demons and anointed with oil many who were sick and healed them.

6a. Greek *chiton*, a long garment worn under the cloak next to the skin

The Death of John the Baptist

¹⁴ King Herod heard of it, for Jesus'[b] name had become known. Some[c] said, "John the Baptist[d] has been raised from the dead. That is why these miraculous powers are at work in him." ¹⁵ But others said, "He is Elijah." And others said, "He is a prophet, like one of the prophets of old." ¹⁶ But when Herod heard of it, he said, "John, whom I beheaded, has been raised." ¹⁷ For it was Herod who had sent and seized John and bound him in prison for the sake of Herodias, his brother Philip's wife, because he had married her. ¹⁸ For John had been saying to Herod, "It is not lawful for you to have your brother's wife." ¹⁹ And Herodias had a grudge against him and wanted to put him to death. But she could not, ²⁰ for Herod feared John, knowing that he was a righteous and holy man, and he kept him safe. When he heard him, he was greatly perplexed, and yet he heard him gladly.

²¹ But an opportunity came when Herod on his birthday gave a banquet for his nobles and military commanders and the leading men of Galilee. ²² For when Herodias's daughter came in and danced, she pleased Herod and his guests. And the king said to the girl, "Ask me for whatever you wish, and I will give it to you." ²³ And he vowed to her, "Whatever you ask me, I will give

---

6b. Greek *his*
6c. Some manuscripts *He*
6d. Greek *baptizer*; also verse 24

you, up to half of my kingdom." ²⁴ And she went out and said to her mother, "For what should I ask?" And she said, "The head of John the Baptist." ²⁵ And she came in immediately with haste to the king and asked, saying, "I want you to give me at once the head of John the Baptist on a platter." ²⁶ And the king was exceedingly sorry, but because of his oaths and his guests he did not want to break his word to her. ²⁷ And immediately the king sent an executioner with orders to bring John's*ᵉ* head. He went and beheaded him in the prison ²⁸ and brought his head on a platter and gave it to the girl, and the girl gave it to her mother. ²⁹ When his disciples heard of it, they came and took his body and laid it in a tomb.

Jesus Feeds the Five Thousand

³⁰ The apostles returned to Jesus and told him all that they had done and taught. ³¹ And he said to them, "Come away by yourselves to a desolate place and rest a while." For many were coming and going, and they had no leisure even to eat. ³² And they went away in the boat to a desolate place by themselves. ³³ Now many saw them going and recognized them, and they ran there on foot from all the towns and got there ahead of them. ³⁴ When he went ashore he saw a great crowd, and he had compassion on them, because they were like sheep

---

⁶ᵉ Greek *his*

without a shepherd. And he began to teach them many things. ³⁵ And when it grew late, his disciples came to him and said, "This is a desolate place, and the hour is now late. ³⁶ Send them away to go into the surrounding countryside and villages and buy themselves something to eat." ³⁷ But he answered them, "You give them something to eat." And they said to him, "Shall we go and buy two hundred denarii*f* worth of bread and give it to them to eat?" ³⁸ And he said to them, "How many loaves do you have? Go and see." And when they had found out, they said, "Five, and two fish." ³⁹ Then he commanded them all to sit down in groups on the green grass. ⁴⁰ So they sat down in groups, by hundreds and by fifties. ⁴¹ And taking the five loaves and the two fish, he looked up to heaven and said a blessing and broke the loaves and gave them to the disciples to set before the people. And he divided the two fish among them all. ⁴² And they all ate and were satisfied. ⁴³ And they took up twelve baskets full of broken pieces and of the fish. ⁴⁴ And those who ate the loaves were five thousand men.

Jesus Walks on the Water

⁴⁵ Immediately he made his disciples get into the boat and go before him to the other side, to Bethsaida, while he dismissed the crowd. ⁴⁶ And after he had taken leave of

---

6*f*. A *denarius* was a day's wage for a labourer

them, he went up on the mountain to pray. ⁴⁷ And when evening came, the boat was out on the sea, and he was alone on the land. ⁴⁸ And he saw that they were making headway painfully, for the wind was against them. And about the fourth watch of the night[g] he came to them, walking on the sea. He meant to pass by them, ⁴⁹ but when they saw him walking on the sea they thought it was a ghost, and cried out, ⁵⁰ for they all saw him and were terrified. But immediately he spoke to them and said, "Take heart; it is I. Do not be afraid." ⁵¹ And he got into the boat with them, and the wind ceased. And they were utterly astounded, ⁵² for they did not understand about the loaves, but their hearts were hardened.

Jesus Heals the Sick in Gennesaret

⁵³ When they had crossed over, they came to land at Gennesaret and moored to the shore. ⁵⁴ And when they got out of the boat, the people immediately recognized him ⁵⁵ and ran about the whole region and began to bring the sick people on their beds to wherever they heard he was. ⁵⁶ And wherever he came, in villages, cities, or countryside, they laid the sick in the market-places and implored him that they might touch even the fringe of his garment. And as many as touched it were made well.

---

[g] That is, between 3 a.m. and 6 a.m.

Traditions and Commandments

7 Now when the Pharisees gathered to him, with some of the scribes who had come from Jerusalem, ² they saw that some of his disciples ate with hands that were defiled, that is, unwashed. ³ (For the Pharisees and all the Jews do not eat unless they wash their hands properly,[a] holding to the tradition of the elders, ⁴ and when they come from the market-place, they do not eat unless they wash.[b] And there are many other traditions that they observe, such as the washing of cups and pots and copper vessels and dining couches.[c]) ⁵ And the Pharisees and the scribes asked him, "Why do your disciples not walk according to the tradition of the elders, but eat with defiled hands?" ⁶ And he said to them, "Well did Isaiah prophesy of you hypocrites, as it is written,

> "'This people honours me with their lips,
>   but their heart is far from me;
> ⁷ in vain do they worship me,
>   teaching as doctrines the commandments of men.'

⁸ You leave the commandment of God and hold to the tradition of men."

[7a.] Greek *unless they wash the hands with a fist*, probably indicating a kind of ceremonial washing

[7b.] Greek *unless they baptize*; some manuscripts *unless they purify themselves*

[7c.] Some manuscripts omit *and dining couches*

⁹ And he said to them, "You have a fine way of rejecting the commandment of God in order to establish your tradition! ¹⁰ For Moses said, 'Honour your father and your mother'; and, 'Whoever reviles father or mother must surely die.' ¹¹ But you say, 'If a man tells his father or his mother, "Whatever you would have gained from me is Corban"' (that is, given to God)[d] – ¹² then you no longer permit him to do anything for his father or mother, ¹³ thus making void the word of God by your tradition that you have handed down. And many such things you do."

What Defiles a Person

¹⁴ And he called the people to him again and said to them, "Hear me, all of you, and understand: ¹⁵ There is nothing outside a person that by going into him can defile him, but the things that come out of a person are what defile him."[e] ¹⁷ And when he had entered the house and left the people, his disciples asked him about the parable. ¹⁸ And he said to them, "Then are you also without understanding? Do you not see that whatever goes into a person from outside cannot defile him, ¹⁹ since it enters not his heart but his stomach, and is expelled?"[f] (Thus he declared all foods clean.) ²⁰ And he

---

7d. Or *an offering*
7e. Some manuscripts add verse 16: *If anyone has ears to hear, let him hear*
7f. Greek *goes out into the latrine*

said, "What comes out of a person is what defiles him. ²¹ For from within, out of the heart of man, come evil thoughts, sexual immorality, theft, murder, adultery, ²² coveting, wickedness, deceit, sensuality, envy, slander, pride, foolishness. ²³ All these evil things come from within, and they defile a person."

The Syrophoenician Woman's Faith

²⁴ And from there he arose and went away to the region of Tyre and Sidon.ᵍ And he entered a house and did not want anyone to know, yet he could not be hidden. ²⁵ But immediately a woman whose little daughter had an unclean spirit heard of him and came and fell down at his feet. ²⁶ Now the woman was a Gentile, a Syrophoenician by birth. And she begged him to cast the demon out of her daughter. ²⁷ And he said to her, "Let the children be fed first, for it is not right to take the children's bread and throw it to the dogs." ²⁸ But she answered him, "Yes, Lord; yet even the dogs under the table eat the children's crumbs." ²⁹ And he said to her, "For this statement you may go your way; the demon has left your daughter." ³⁰ And she went home and found the child lying in bed and the demon gone.

7ᵍ· Some manuscripts omit *and Sidon*

Jesus Heals a Deaf Man

³¹ Then he returned from the region of Tyre and went through Sidon to the Sea of Galilee, in the region of the Decapolis. ³² And they brought to him a man who was deaf and had a speech impediment, and they begged him to lay his hand on him. ³³ And taking him aside from the crowd privately, he put his fingers into his ears, and after spitting touched his tongue. ³⁴ And looking up to heaven, he sighed and said to him, "Ephphatha", that is, "Be opened." ³⁵ And his ears were opened, his tongue was released, and he spoke plainly. ³⁶ And Jesus*ʰ* charged them to tell no one. But the more he charged them, the more zealously they proclaimed it. ³⁷ And they were astonished beyond measure, saying, "He has done all things well. He even makes the deaf hear and the mute speak."

Jesus Feeds the Four Thousand

8 In those days, when again a great crowd had gathered, and they had nothing to eat, he called his disciples to him and said to them, ² "I have compassion on the crowd, because they have been with me now three days and have nothing to eat. ³ And if I send them away hungry to their homes, they will faint on the way. And some of them have come from far away." ⁴ And his disciples answered him, "How can one feed these people

---

⁷*ʰ*. Greek *he*

with bread here in this desolate place?" ⁵ And he asked them, "How many loaves do you have?" They said, "Seven." ⁶ And he directed the crowd to sit down on the ground. And he took the seven loaves, and having given thanks, he broke them and gave them to his disciples to set before the people; and they set them before the crowd. ⁷ And they had a few small fish. And having blessed them, he said that these also should be set before them. ⁸ And they ate and were satisfied. And they took up the broken pieces left over, seven baskets full. ⁹ And there were about four thousand people. And he sent them away. ¹⁰ And immediately he got into the boat with his disciples and went to the district of Dalmanutha.[a]

The Pharisees Demand a Sign

¹¹ The Pharisees came and began to argue with him, seeking from him a sign from heaven to test him. ¹² And he sighed deeply in his spirit and said, "Why does this generation seek a sign? Truly, I say to you, no sign will be given to this generation." ¹³ And he left them, got into the boat again, and went to the other side.

The Leaven of the Pharisees and Herod

¹⁴ Now they had forgotten to bring bread, and they had only one loaf with them in the boat. ¹⁵ And he cautioned

---

8a. Some manuscripts *Magadan*, or *Magdala*

them, saying, "Watch out; beware of the leaven of the Pharisees and the leaven of Herod."[b] ¹⁶ And they began discussing with one another the fact that they had no bread. ¹⁷ And Jesus, aware of this, said to them, "Why are you discussing the fact that you have no bread? Do you not yet perceive or understand? Are your hearts hardened? ¹⁸ Having eyes do you not see, and having ears do you not hear? And do you not remember? ¹⁹ When I broke the five loaves for the five thousand, how many baskets full of broken pieces did you take up?" They said to him, "Twelve." ²⁰ "And the seven for the four thousand, how many baskets full of broken pieces did you take up?" And they said to him, "Seven." ²¹ And he said to them, "Do you not yet understand?"

Jesus Heals a Blind Man at Bethsaida

²² And they came to Bethsaida. And some people brought to him a blind man and begged him to touch him. ²³ And he took the blind man by the hand and led him out of the village, and when he had spat on his eyes and laid his hands on him, he asked him, "Do you see anything?" ²⁴ And he looked up and said, "I see people, but they look like trees, walking." ²⁵ Then Jesus[c] laid his hands on his eyes again; and he opened his eyes, his sight was restored, and he saw everything clearly.

8b. Some manuscripts *the Herodians*
8c. Greek *he*

²⁶ And he sent him to his home, saying, "Do not even enter the village."

Peter Confesses Jesus as the Christ

²⁷ And Jesus went on with his disciples to the villages of Caesarea Philippi. And on the way he asked his disciples, "Who do people say that I am?" ²⁸ And they told him, "John the Baptist; and others say, Elijah; and others, one of the prophets." ²⁹ And he asked them, "But who do you say that I am?" Peter answered him, "You are the Christ." ³⁰ And he strictly charged them to tell no one about him.

Jesus Foretells His Death and Resurrection

³¹ And he began to teach them that the Son of Man must suffer many things and be rejected by the elders and the chief priests and the scribes and be killed, and after three days rise again. ³² And he said this plainly. And Peter took him aside and began to rebuke him. ³³ But turning and seeing his disciples, he rebuked Peter and said, "Get behind me, Satan! For you are not setting your mind on the things of God, but on the things of man."

³⁴ And calling the crowd to him with his disciples, he said to them, "If anyone would come after me, let him deny himself and take up his cross and follow me. ³⁵ For whoever would save his life[d] will lose it, but whoever

---

[8d] The same Greek word can mean either *soul* or *life*, depending on the context; twice in this verse and once in verse 36 and once in verse 37

loses his life for my sake and the gospel's will save it. ³⁶ For what does it profit a man to gain the whole world and forfeit his soul? ³⁷ For what can a man give in return for his soul? ³⁸ For whoever is ashamed of me and of my words in this adulterous and sinful generation, of him will the Son of Man also be ashamed when he comes in the glory of his Father with the holy angels."

9 And he said to them, "Truly, I say to you, there are some standing here who will not taste death until they see the kingdom of God after it has come with power."

The Transfiguration

² And after six days Jesus took with him Peter and James and John, and led them up a high mountain by themselves. And he was transfigured before them, ³ and his clothes became radiant, intensely white, as no one*a* on earth could bleach them. ⁴ And there appeared to them Elijah with Moses, and they were talking with Jesus. ⁵ And Peter said to Jesus, "Rabbi,*b* it is good that we are here. Let us make three tents, one for you and one for Moses and one for Elijah." ⁶ For he did not know what to say, for they were terrified. ⁷ And a cloud overshadowed them, and a voice came out of the cloud, "This is my beloved

---

9a. Greek *launderer* (*gnapheus*)
9b. *Rabbi* means *my teacher*, or *my master*

Son;*c* listen to him." ⁸ And suddenly, looking around, they no longer saw anyone with them but Jesus only.

⁹ And as they were coming down the mountain, he charged them to tell no one what they had seen, until the Son of Man had risen from the dead. ¹⁰ So they kept the matter to themselves, questioning what this rising from the dead might mean. ¹¹ And they asked him, "Why do the scribes say that first Elijah must come?" ¹² And he said to them, "Elijah does come first to restore all things. And how is it written of the Son of Man that he should suffer many things and be treated with contempt? ¹³ But I tell you that Elijah has come, and they did to him whatever they pleased, as it is written of him."

Jesus Heals a Boy with an Unclean Spirit

¹⁴ And when they came to the disciples, they saw a great crowd around them, and scribes arguing with them. ¹⁵ And immediately all the crowd, when they saw him, were greatly amazed and ran up to him and greeted him. ¹⁶ And he asked them, "What are you arguing about with them?" ¹⁷ And someone from the crowd answered him, "Teacher, I brought my son to you, for he has a spirit that makes him mute. ¹⁸ And whenever it seizes him, it throws him down, and he foams and grinds his teeth and becomes rigid. So I asked your disciples to

---

9c. Or *my Son, my* (or *the*) *Beloved*

cast it out, and they were not able." ¹⁹ And he answered them, "O faithless generation, how long am I to be with you? How long am I to bear with you? Bring him to me." ²⁰ And they brought the boy to him. And when the spirit saw him, immediately it convulsed the boy, and he fell on the ground and rolled about, foaming at the mouth. ²¹ And Jesus asked his father, "How long has this been happening to him?" And he said, "From childhood. ²² And it has often cast him into fire and into water, to destroy him. But if you can do anything, have compassion on us and help us." ²³ And Jesus said to him, "'If you can'! All things are possible for one who believes." ²⁴ Immediately the father of the child cried out*ᵈ* and said, "I believe; help my unbelief!" ²⁵ And when Jesus saw that a crowd came running together, he rebuked the unclean spirit, saying to it, "You mute and deaf spirit, I command you, come out of him and never enter him again." ²⁶ And after crying out and convulsing him terribly, it came out, and the boy was like a corpse, so that most of them said, "He is dead." ²⁷ But Jesus took him by the hand and lifted him up, and he arose. ²⁸ And when he had entered the house, his disciples asked him privately, "Why could we not cast it out?" ²⁹ And he said to them, "This kind cannot be driven out by anything but prayer."*ᵉ*

9d. Some manuscripts add *with tears*
9e. Some manuscripts add *and fasting*

Jesus Again Foretells Death, Resurrection

30 They went on from there and passed through Galilee. And he did not want anyone to know, 31 for he was teaching his disciples, saying to them, "The Son of Man is going to be delivered into the hands of men, and they will kill him. And when he is killed, after three days he will rise." 32 But they did not understand the saying, and were afraid to ask him.

Who Is the Greatest?

33 And they came to Capernaum. And when he was in the house he asked them, "What were you discussing on the way?" 34 But they kept silent, for on the way they had argued with one another about who was the greatest. 35 And he sat down and called the twelve. And he said to them, "If anyone would be first, he must be last of all and servant of all." 36 And he took a child and put him in the midst of them, and taking him in his arms, he said to them, 37 "Whoever receives one such child in my name receives me, and whoever receives me, receives not me but him who sent me."

Anyone Not Against Us Is for Us

38 John said to him, "Teacher, we saw someone casting out demons in your name,*f* and we tried to stop him, because he was not following us." 39 But Jesus said, "Do

---

9*f.* Some manuscripts add *who does not follow us*

not stop him, for no one who does a mighty work in my name will be able soon afterwards to speak evil of me. ⁴⁰ For the one who is not against us is for us. ⁴¹ For truly, I say to you, whoever gives you a cup of water to drink because you belong to Christ will by no means lose his reward.

Temptations to Sin

⁴² "Whoever causes one of these little ones who believe in me to sin,ᵍ it would be better for him if a great millstone were hung round his neck and he were thrown into the sea. ⁴³ And if your hand causes you to sin, cut it off. It is better for you to enter life crippled than with two hands to go to hell,ʰ to the unquenchable fire.ⁱ ⁴⁵ And if your foot causes you to sin, cut it off. It is better for you to enter life lame than with two feet to be thrown into hell. ⁴⁷ And if your eye causes you to sin, tear it out. It is better for you to enter the kingdom of God with one eye than with two eyes to be thrown into hell, ⁴⁸ 'where their worm does not die and the fire is not quenched.' ⁴⁹ For everyone will be salted with fire.ʲ ⁵⁰ Salt is good, but if the salt has lost its saltiness, how will you make it salty again? Have salt in yourselves, and be at peace with one another."

9g. Greek *to stumble*; also verses 43, 45, 47
9h. Greek *Gehenna*; also verse 47
9i. Some manuscripts add verses 44 and 46 (which are identical with verse 48)
9j. Some manuscripts add *and every sacrifice will be salted with salt*

Teaching About Divorce

10 And he left there and went to the region of Judea and beyond the Jordan, and crowds gathered to him again. And again, as was his custom, he taught them.

² And Pharisees came up and in order to test him asked, "Is it lawful for a man to divorce his wife?" ³ He answered them, "What did Moses command you?" ⁴ They said, "Moses allowed a man to write a certificate of divorce and to send her away." ⁵ And Jesus said to them, "Because of your hardness of heart he wrote you this commandment. ⁶ But from the beginning of creation, 'God made them male and female.' ⁷ 'Therefore a man shall leave his father and mother and hold fast to his wife,[a] ⁸ and the two shall become one flesh.' So they are no longer two but one flesh. ⁹ What therefore God has joined together, let not man separate."

¹⁰ And in the house the disciples asked him again about this matter. ¹¹ And he said to them, "Whoever divorces his wife and marries another commits adultery against her, ¹² and if she divorces her husband and marries another, she commits adultery."

Let the Children Come to Me

¹³ And they were bringing children to him that he might touch them, and the disciples rebuked them. ¹⁴ But when Jesus saw it, he was indignant and said to them,

---

[10a.] Some manuscripts omit *and hold fast to his wife*

"Let the children come to me; do not hinder them, for to such belongs the kingdom of God. ¹⁵ Truly, I say to you, whoever does not receive the kingdom of God like a child shall not enter it." ¹⁶ And he took them in his arms and blessed them, laying his hands on them.

The Rich Young Man

¹⁷ And as he was setting out on his journey, a man ran up and knelt before him and asked him, "Good Teacher, what must I do to inherit eternal life?" ¹⁸ And Jesus said to him, "Why do you call me good? No one is good except God alone. ¹⁹ You know the commandments: 'Do not murder, Do not commit adultery, Do not steal, Do not bear false witness, Do not defraud, Honour your father and mother.'" ²⁰ And he said to him, "Teacher, all these I have kept from my youth." ²¹ And Jesus, looking at him, loved him, and said to him, "You lack one thing: go, sell all that you have and give to the poor, and you will have treasure in heaven; and come, follow me." ²² Disheartened by the saying, he went away sorrowful, for he had great possessions.

²³ And Jesus looked around and said to his disciples, "How difficult it will be for those who have wealth to enter the kingdom of God!" ²⁴ And the disciples were amazed at his words. But Jesus said to them again, "Children, how difficult it is[b] to enter the kingdom of

---

10b. Some manuscripts add *for those who trust in riches*

God! ²⁵ It is easier for a camel to go through the eye of a needle than for a rich person to enter the kingdom of God." ²⁶ And they were exceedingly astonished, and said to him,*c* "Then who can be saved?" ²⁷ Jesus looked at them and said, "With man it is impossible, but not with God. For all things are possible with God." ²⁸ Peter began to say to him, "See, we have left everything and followed you." ²⁹ Jesus said, "Truly, I say to you, there is no one who has left house or brothers or sisters or mother or father or children or lands, for my sake and for the gospel, ³⁰ who will not receive a hundredfold now in this time, houses and brothers and sisters and mothers and children and lands, with persecutions, and in the age to come eternal life. ³¹ But many who are first will be last, and the last first."

Jesus Foretells His Death a Third Time

³² And they were on the road, going up to Jerusalem, and Jesus was walking ahead of them. And they were amazed, and those who followed were afraid. And taking the twelve again, he began to tell them what was to happen to him, ³³ saying, "See, we are going up to Jerusalem, and the Son of Man will be delivered over to the chief priests and the scribes, and they will condemn him to death and deliver him over to the Gentiles. ³⁴ And

---

10c. Some manuscripts *to one another*

they will mock him and spit on him, and flog him and kill him. And after three days he will rise."

The Request of James and John

³⁵ And James and John, the sons of Zebedee, came up to him and said to him, "Teacher, we want you to do for us whatever we ask of you." ³⁶ And he said to them, "What do you want me to do for you?" ³⁷ And they said to him, "Grant us to sit, one at your right hand and one at your left, in your glory." ³⁸ Jesus said to them, "You do not know what you are asking. Are you able to drink the cup that I drink, or to be baptized with the baptism with which I am baptized?" ³⁹ And they said to him, "We are able." And Jesus said to them, "The cup that I drink you will drink, and with the baptism with which I am baptized, you will be baptized, ⁴⁰ but to sit at my right hand or at my left is not mine to grant, but it is for those for whom it has been prepared." ⁴¹ And when the ten heard it, they began to be indignant at James and John. ⁴² And Jesus called them to him and said to them, "You know that those who are considered rulers of the Gentiles lord it over them, and their great ones exercise authority over them. ⁴³ But it shall not be so among you. But whoever would be great among you must be your servant,*ᵈ* ⁴⁴ and whoever would be first among you must

---

10d. Greek *diakonos*

be slave[e] of all. ⁴⁵ For even the Son of Man came not to be served but to serve, and to give his life as a ransom for many."

Jesus Heals Blind Bartimaeus

⁴⁶ And they came to Jericho. And as he was leaving Jericho with his disciples and a great crowd, Bartimaeus, a blind beggar, the son of Timaeus, was sitting by the roadside. ⁴⁷ And when he heard that it was Jesus of Nazareth, he began to cry out and say, "Jesus, Son of David, have mercy on me!" ⁴⁸ And many rebuked him, telling him to be silent. But he cried out all the more, "Son of David, have mercy on me!" ⁴⁹ And Jesus stopped and said, "Call him." And they called the blind man, saying to him, "Take heart. Get up; he is calling you." ⁵⁰ And throwing off his cloak, he sprang up and came to Jesus. ⁵¹ And Jesus said to him, "What do you want me to do for you?" And the blind man said to him, "Rabbi, let me recover my sight." ⁵² And Jesus said to him, "Go your way; your faith has made you well." And immediately he recovered his sight and followed him on the way.

The Triumphal Entry

11 Now when they drew near to Jerusalem, to Bethphage and Bethany, at the Mount of Olives,

---

10e. Or *bondservant*, or *servant*

Jesus[a] sent two of his disciples ²and said to them, "Go into the village in front of you, and immediately as you enter it you will find a colt tied, on which no one has ever sat. Untie it and bring it. ³If anyone says to you, 'Why are you doing this?' say, 'The Lord has need of it and will send it back here immediately.'" ⁴And they went away and found a colt tied at a door outside in the street, and they untied it. ⁵And some of those standing there said to them, "What are you doing, untying the colt?" ⁶And they told them what Jesus had said, and they let them go. ⁷And they brought the colt to Jesus and threw their cloaks on it, and he sat on it. ⁸And many spread their cloaks on the road, and others spread leafy branches that they had cut from the fields. ⁹And those who went before and those who followed were shouting, "Hosanna! Blessed is he who comes in the name of the Lord! ¹⁰Blessed is the coming kingdom of our father David! Hosanna in the highest!"

¹¹And he entered Jerusalem and went into the temple. And when he had looked around at everything, as it was already late, he went out to Bethany with the twelve.

Jesus Curses the Fig Tree

¹²On the following day, when they came from Bethany, he was hungry. ¹³And seeing in the distance a fig tree in leaf, he went to see if he could find anything on it. When

---

11a Greek *he*

he came to it, he found nothing but leaves, for it was not the season for figs. ¹⁴ And he said to it, "May no one ever eat fruit from you again." And his disciples heard it.

Jesus Cleanses the Temple

¹⁵ And they came to Jerusalem. And he entered the temple and began to drive out those who sold and those who bought in the temple, and he overturned the tables of the money-changers and the seats of those who sold pigeons. ¹⁶ And he would not allow anyone to carry anything through the temple. ¹⁷ And he was teaching them and saying to them, "Is it not written, 'My house shall be called a house of prayer for all the nations'? But you have made it a den of robbers." ¹⁸ And the chief priests and the scribes heard it and were seeking a way to destroy him, for they feared him, because all the crowd was astonished at his teaching. ¹⁹ And when evening came they[b] went out of the city.

The Lesson from the Withered Fig Tree

²⁰ As they passed by in the morning, they saw the fig tree withered away to its roots. ²¹ And Peter remembered and said to him, "Rabbi, look! The fig tree that you cursed has withered." ²² And Jesus answered them, "Have faith in God. ²³ Truly, I say to you, whoever says to this mountain, 'Be taken up and thrown into the sea', and

---

11b. Some manuscripts *he*

does not doubt in his heart, but believes that what he says will come to pass, it will be done for him. ²⁴ Therefore I tell you, whatever you ask in prayer, believe that you have received*c* it, and it will be yours. ²⁵ And whenever you stand praying, forgive, if you have anything against anyone, so that your Father also who is in heaven may forgive you your trespasses."*d*

The Authority of Jesus Challenged

²⁷ And they came again to Jerusalem. And as he was walking in the temple, the chief priests and the scribes and the elders came to him, ²⁸ and they said to him, "By what authority are you doing these things, or who gave you this authority to do them?" ²⁹ Jesus said to them, "I will ask you one question; answer me, and I will tell you by what authority I do these things. ³⁰ Was the baptism of John from heaven or from man? Answer me." ³¹ And they discussed it with one another, saying, "If we say, 'From heaven', he will say, 'Why then did you not believe him?' ³² But shall we say, 'From man'?" – they were afraid of the people, for they all held that John really was a prophet. ³³ So they answered Jesus, "We do not know." And Jesus said to them, "Neither will I tell you by what authority I do these things."

11c. Some manuscripts *are receiving*
11d. Some manuscripts add verse 26: *But if you do not forgive, neither will your Father who is in heaven forgive your trespasses*

The Parable of the Tenants

12 And he began to speak to them in parables. "A man planted a vineyard and put a fence around it and dug a pit for the wine press and built a tower, and leased it to tenants and went into another country. ² When the season came, he sent a servant[a] to the tenants to get from them some of the fruit of the vineyard. ³ And they took him and beat him and sent him away empty-handed. ⁴ Again he sent to them another servant, and they struck him on the head and treated him shamefully. ⁵ And he sent another, and him they killed. And so with many others: some they beat, and some they killed. ⁶ He had still one other, a beloved son. Finally he sent him to them, saying, 'They will respect my son.' ⁷ But those tenants said to one another, 'This is the heir. Come, let us kill him, and the inheritance will be ours.' ⁸ And they took him and killed him and threw him out of the vineyard. ⁹ What will the owner of the vineyard do? He will come and destroy the tenants and give the vineyard to others. ¹⁰ Have you not read this Scripture:

"'The stone that the builders rejected
    has become the cornerstone;[b]
¹¹   this was the Lord's doing,
    and it is marvellous in our eyes'?"

[12a.] Or *bondservant*; also verse 4
[12b.] Greek *the head of the corner*

¹² And they were seeking to arrest him but feared the people, for they perceived that he had told the parable against them. So they left him and went away.

Paying Taxes to Caesar

¹³ And they sent to him some of the Pharisees and some of the Herodians, to trap him in his talk. ¹⁴ And they came and said to him, "Teacher, we know that you are true and do not care about anyone's opinion. For you are not swayed by appearances,[c] but truly teach the way of God. Is it lawful to pay taxes to Caesar, or not? Should we pay them, or should we not?" ¹⁵ But, knowing their hypocrisy, he said to them, "Why put me to the test? Bring me a denarius[d] and let me look at it." ¹⁶ And they brought one. And he said to them, "Whose likeness and inscription is this?" They said to him, "Caesar's." ¹⁷ Jesus said to them, "Render to Caesar the things that are Caesar's, and to God the things that are God's." And they marvelled at him.

The Sadducees Ask About the Resurrection

¹⁸ And Sadducees came to him, who say that there is no resurrection. And they asked him a question, saying, ¹⁹ "Teacher, Moses wrote for us that if a man's brother dies

---

12c. Greek *you do not look at people's faces*
12d. A *denarius* was a day's wage for a labourer

and leaves a wife, but leaves no child, the man[e] must take the widow and raise up offspring for his brother. ²⁰ There were seven brothers; the first took a wife, and when he died left no offspring. ²¹ And the second took her, and died, leaving no offspring. And the third likewise. ²² And the seven left no offspring. Last of all the woman also died. ²³ In the resurrection, when they rise again, whose wife will she be? For the seven had her as wife."

²⁴ Jesus said to them, "Is this not the reason you are wrong, because you know neither the Scriptures nor the power of God? ²⁵ For when they rise from the dead, they neither marry nor are given in marriage, but are like angels in heaven. ²⁶ And as for the dead being raised, have you not read in the book of Moses, in the passage about the bush, how God spoke to him, saying, 'I am the God of Abraham, and the God of Isaac, and the God of Jacob'? ²⁷ He is not God of the dead, but of the living. You are quite wrong."

The Great Commandment

²⁸ And one of the scribes came up and heard them disputing with one another, and seeing that he answered them well, asked him, "Which commandment is the most important of all?" ²⁹ Jesus answered, "The most important is, 'Hear, O Israel: The Lord our God, the Lord is one. ³⁰ And you shall love the Lord your God

---

12e. Greek *his brother*

with all your heart and with all your soul and with all your mind and with all your strength.' ³¹ The second is this: 'You shall love your neighbour as yourself.' There is no other commandment greater than these." ³² And the scribe said to him, "You are right, Teacher. You have truly said that he is one, and there is no other besides him. ³³ And to love him with all the heart and with all the understanding and with all the strength, and to love one's neighbour as oneself, is much more than all whole burnt offerings and sacrifices." ³⁴ And when Jesus saw that he answered wisely, he said to him, "You are not far from the kingdom of God." And after that no one dared to ask him any more questions.

Whose Son Is the Christ?

³⁵ And as Jesus taught in the temple, he said, "How can the scribes say that the Christ is the son of David? ³⁶ David himself, in the Holy Spirit, declared,

" 'The Lord said to my Lord,
  'Sit at my right hand,
    until I put your enemies under your feet.' '

³⁷ David himself calls him Lord. So how is he his son?" And the great throng heard him gladly.

Beware of the Scribes

³⁸ And in his teaching he said, "Beware of the scribes, who like to walk around in long robes and like greetings

in the market-places ³⁹ and have the best seats in the synagogues and the places of honour at feasts, ⁴⁰ who devour widows' houses and for a pretence make long prayers. They will receive the greater condemnation."

The Widow's Offering

⁴¹ And he sat down opposite the treasury and watched the people putting money into the offering box. Many rich people put in large sums. ⁴² And a poor widow came and put in two small copper coins, which make a penny.*ᶠ* ⁴³ And he called his disciples to him and said to them, "Truly, I say to you, this poor widow has put in more than all those who are contributing to the offering box. ⁴⁴ For they all contributed out of their abundance, but she out of her poverty has put in everything she had, all she had to live on."

Jesus Foretells Destruction of the Temple

13 And as he came out of the temple, one of his disciples said to him, "Look, Teacher, what wonderful stones and what wonderful buildings!" ² And Jesus said to him, "Do you see these great buildings? There will not be left here one stone upon another that will not be thrown down."

12f. Greek *two lepta*, which make a *kodrantes*; a *kodrantes* (Latin *quadrans*) was a Roman copper coin worth about ¹/₆₄ of a *denarius* (which was a day's wage for a labourer)

Signs of the End of the Age

³ And as he sat on the Mount of Olives opposite the temple, Peter and James and John and Andrew asked him privately, ⁴ "Tell us, when will these things be, and what will be the sign when all these things are about to be accomplished?" ⁵ And Jesus began to say to them, "See that no one leads you astray. ⁶ Many will come in my name, saying, 'I am he!' and they will lead many astray. ⁷ And when you hear of wars and rumours of wars, do not be alarmed. This must take place, but the end is not yet. ⁸ For nation will rise against nation, and kingdom against kingdom. There will be earthquakes in various places; there will be famines. These are but the beginning of the birth pains.

⁹ "But be on your guard. For they will deliver you over to councils, and you will be beaten in synagogues, and you will stand before governors and kings for my sake, to bear witness before them. ¹⁰ And the gospel must first be proclaimed to all nations. ¹¹ And when they bring you to trial and deliver you over, do not be anxious beforehand what you are to say, but say whatever is given you in that hour, for it is not you who speak, but the Holy Spirit. ¹² And brother will deliver brother over to death, and the father his child, and children will rise against parents and have them put to death. ¹³ And you will be hated by all for my name's sake. But the one who endures to the end will be saved.

The Abomination of Desolation

¹⁴ "But when you see the abomination of desolation standing where he ought not to be (let the reader understand), then let those who are in Judea flee to the mountains. ¹⁵ Let the one who is on the housetop not go down, nor enter his house, to take anything out, ¹⁶ and let the one who is in the field not turn back to take his cloak. ¹⁷ And alas for women who are pregnant and for those who are nursing infants in those days! ¹⁸ Pray that it may not happen in winter. ¹⁹ For in those days there will be such tribulation as has not been from the beginning of the creation that God created until now, and never will be. ²⁰ And if the Lord had not cut short the days, no human being would be saved. But for the sake of the elect, whom he chose, he shortened the days. ²¹ And then if anyone says to you, 'Look, here is the Christ!' or 'Look, there he is!' do not believe it. ²² For false christs and false prophets will arise and perform signs and wonders, to lead astray, if possible, the elect. ²³ But be on guard; I have told you all things beforehand.

The Coming of the Son of Man

²⁴ "But in those days, after that tribulation, the sun will be darkened, and the moon will not give its light, ²⁵ and the stars will be falling from heaven, and the powers in the heavens will be shaken. ²⁶ And then they will see the Son of Man coming in clouds with great power and glory. ²⁷ And then he will send out the angels and gather

his elect from the four winds, from the ends of the earth to the ends of heaven.

The Lesson of the Fig Tree

²⁸ "From the fig tree learn its lesson: as soon as its branch becomes tender and puts out its leaves, you know that summer is near. ²⁹ So also, when you see these things taking place, you know that he is near, at the very gates. ³⁰ Truly, I say to you, this generation will not pass away until all these things take place. ³¹ Heaven and earth will pass away, but my words will not pass away.

No One Knows That Day or Hour

³² "But concerning that day or that hour, no one knows, not even the angels in heaven, nor the Son, but only the Father. ³³ Be on guard, keep awake.[a] For you do not know when the time will come. ³⁴ It is like a man going on a journey, when he leaves home and puts his servants[b] in charge, each with his work, and commands the doorkeeper to stay awake. ³⁵ Therefore stay awake – for you do not know when the master of the house will come, in the evening, or at midnight, or when the cock crows,[c] or in the morning – ³⁶ lest he come suddenly

---

13a. Some manuscripts add *and pray*
13b. Or *bondservants*
13c. That is, the third watch of the night, between midnight and 3 a.m.

and find you asleep. ³⁷ And what I say to you I say to all: Stay awake."

The Plot to Kill Jesus

14 It was now two days before the Passover and the Feast of Unleavened Bread. And the chief priests and the scribes were seeking how to arrest him by stealth and kill him, ² for they said, "Not during the feast, lest there be an uproar from the people."

Jesus Anointed at Bethany

³ And while he was at Bethany in the house of Simon the leper,ᵃ as he was reclining at table, a woman came with an alabaster flask of ointment of pure nard, very costly, and she broke the flask and poured it over his head. ⁴ There were some who said to themselves indignantly, "Why was the ointment wasted like that? ⁵ For this ointment could have been sold for more than three hundred denariiᵇ and given to the poor." And they scolded her. ⁶ But Jesus said, "Leave her alone. Why do you trouble her? She has done a beautiful thing to me. ⁷ For you always have the poor with you, and whenever you want, you can do good for them. But you will not always have me. ⁸ She has done what she could; she has anointed my body beforehand for burial. ⁹ And truly,

---

14a. *Leprosy* was a term for several skin diseases; see Leviticus 13
14b. A *denarius* was a day's wage for a labourer

I say to you, wherever the gospel is proclaimed in the whole world, what she has done will be told in memory of her."

Judas to Betray Jesus

¹⁰ Then Judas Iscariot, who was one of the twelve, went to the chief priests in order to betray him to them. ¹¹ And when they heard it, they were glad and promised to give him money. And he sought an opportunity to betray him.

The Passover with the Disciples

¹² And on the first day of Unleavened Bread, when they sacrificed the Passover lamb, his disciples said to him, "Where will you have us go and prepare for you to eat the Passover?" ¹³ And he sent two of his disciples and said to them, "Go into the city, and a man carrying a jar of water will meet you. Follow him, ¹⁴ and wherever he enters, say to the master of the house, 'The Teacher says, Where is my guest room, where I may eat the Passover with my disciples?' ¹⁵ And he will show you a large upper room furnished and ready; there prepare for us." ¹⁶ And the disciples set out and went to the city and found it just as he had told them, and they prepared the Passover.

¹⁷ And when it was evening, he came with the twelve. ¹⁸ And as they were reclining at table and eating, Jesus said, "Truly, I say to you, one of you will betray me, one who is eating with me." ¹⁹ They began to be sorrowful and

to say to him one after another, "Is it I?" ²⁰ He said to them, "It is one of the twelve, one who is dipping bread into the dish with me. ²¹ For the Son of Man goes as it is written of him, but woe to that man by whom the Son of Man is betrayed! It would have been better for that man if he had not been born."

Institution of the Lord's Supper

²² And as they were eating, he took bread, and after blessing it broke it and gave it to them, and said, "Take; this is my body." ²³ And he took a cup, and when he had given thanks he gave it to them, and they all drank of it. ²⁴ And he said to them, "This is my blood of the[c] covenant, which is poured out for many. ²⁵ Truly, I say to you, I will not drink again of the fruit of the vine until that day when I drink it new in the kingdom of God."

Jesus Foretells Peter's Denial

²⁶ And when they had sung a hymn, they went out to the Mount of Olives. ²⁷ And Jesus said to them, "You will all fall away, for it is written, 'I will strike the shepherd, and the sheep will be scattered.' ²⁸ But after I am raised up, I will go before you to Galilee." ²⁹ Peter said to him, "Even though they all fall away, I will not." ³⁰ And Jesus said to him, "Truly, I tell you, this very night, before the cock crows twice, you will deny me three times." ³¹ But he

---

14c. Some manuscripts insert *new*

said emphatically, "If I must die with you, I will not deny you." And they all said the same.

Jesus Prays in Gethsemane

³² And they went to a place called Gethsemane. And he said to his disciples, "Sit here while I pray." ³³ And he took with him Peter and James and John, and began to be greatly distressed and troubled. ³⁴ And he said to them, "My soul is very sorrowful, even to death. Remain here and watch."*ᵈ* ³⁵ And going a little farther, he fell on the ground and prayed that, if it were possible, the hour might pass from him. ³⁶ And he said, "Abba, Father, all things are possible for you. Remove this cup from me. Yet not what I will, but what you will." ³⁷ And he came and found them sleeping, and he said to Peter, "Simon, are you asleep? Could you not watch one hour? ³⁸ Watch and pray that you may not enter into temptation. The spirit indeed is willing, but the flesh is weak." ³⁹ And again he went away and prayed, saying the same words. ⁴⁰ And again he came and found them sleeping, for their eyes were very heavy, and they did not know what to answer him. ⁴¹ And he came the third time and said to them, "Are you still sleeping and taking your rest? It is enough; the hour has come. The Son of Man is betrayed into the hands of sinners. ⁴² Rise, let us be going; see, my betrayer is at hand."

14d. Or *keep awake*; also verses 37, 38

Betrayal and Arrest of Jesus

⁴³ And immediately, while he was still speaking, Judas came, one of the twelve, and with him a crowd with swords and clubs, from the chief priests and the scribes and the elders. ⁴⁴ Now the betrayer had given them a sign, saying, "The one I will kiss is the man. Seize him and lead him away under guard." ⁴⁵ And when he came, he went up to him at once and said, "Rabbi!" And he kissed him. ⁴⁶ And they laid hands on him and seized him. ⁴⁷ But one of those who stood by drew his sword and struck the servant[e] of the high priest and cut off his ear. ⁴⁸ And Jesus said to them, "Have you come out as against a robber, with swords and clubs to capture me? ⁴⁹ Day after day I was with you in the temple teaching, and you did not seize me. But let the Scriptures be fulfilled." ⁵⁰ And they all left him and fled.

A Young Man Flees

⁵¹ And a young man followed him, with nothing but a linen cloth about his body. And they seized him, ⁵² but he left the linen cloth and ran away naked.

Jesus Before the Council

⁵³ And they led Jesus to the high priest. And all the chief priests and the elders and the scribes came together. ⁵⁴ And Peter had followed him at a distance, right into

---

¹⁴ᵉ Or *bondservant*

the courtyard of the high priest. And he was sitting with the guards and warming himself at the fire. ⁵⁵ Now the chief priests and the whole Council*ᶠ* were seeking testimony against Jesus to put him to death, but they found none. ⁵⁶ For many bore false witness against him, but their testimony did not agree. ⁵⁷ And some stood up and bore false witness against him, saying, ⁵⁸ "We heard him say, 'I will destroy this temple that is made with hands, and in three days I will build another, not made with hands.'" ⁵⁹ Yet even about this their testimony did not agree. ⁶⁰ And the high priest stood up in the midst and asked Jesus, "Have you no answer to make? What is it that these men testify against you?"*ᵍ* ⁶¹ But he remained silent and made no answer. Again the high priest asked him, "Are you the Christ, the Son of the Blessed?" ⁶² And Jesus said, "I am, and you will see the Son of Man seated at the right hand of Power, and coming with the clouds of heaven." ⁶³ And the high priest tore his garments and said, "What further witnesses do we need? ⁶⁴ You have heard his blasphemy. What is your decision?" And they all condemned him as deserving death. ⁶⁵ And some began to spit on him and to cover his face and to strike him, saying to him, "Prophesy!" And the guards received him with blows.

14f. Greek *Sanhedrin*

14g. Or *Have you no answer to what these men testify against you?*

Peter Denies Jesus

⁶⁶ And as Peter was below in the courtyard, one of the servant girls of the high priest came, ⁶⁷ and seeing Peter warming himself, she looked at him and said, "You also were with the Nazarene, Jesus." ⁶⁸ But he denied it, saying, "I neither know nor understand what you mean." And he went out into the gateway[h] and the cock crowed.[i] ⁶⁹ And the servant girl saw him and began again to say to the bystanders, "This man is one of them." ⁷⁰ But again he denied it. And after a little while the bystanders again said to Peter, "Certainly you are one of them, for you are a Galilean." ⁷¹ But he began to invoke a curse on himself and to swear, "I do not know this man of whom you speak." ⁷² And immediately the cock crowed a second time. And Peter remembered how Jesus had said to him, "Before the cock crows twice, you will deny me three times." And he broke down and wept.[j]

Jesus Delivered to Pilate

15 And as soon as it was morning, the chief priests held a consultation with the elders and scribes and the whole Council. And they bound Jesus and led him away and delivered him over to Pilate. ² And Pilate asked him, "Are you the King of the Jews?" And he

---

¹⁴ʰ· Or *forecourt*
¹⁴ⁱ Some manuscripts omit *and the cock crowed*
¹⁴ʲ· Or *And when he had thought about it, he wept*

answered him, "You have said so." ³ And the chief priests accused him of many things. ⁴ And Pilate again asked him, "Have you no answer to make? See how many charges they bring against you." ⁵ But Jesus made no further answer, so that Pilate was amazed.

Pilate Delivers Jesus to Be Crucified

⁶ Now at the feast he used to release for them one prisoner for whom they asked. ⁷ And among the rebels in prison, who had committed murder in the insurrection, there was a man called Barabbas. ⁸ And the crowd came up and began to ask Pilate to do as he usually did for them. ⁹ And he answered them, saying, "Do you want me to release for you the King of the Jews?" ¹⁰ For he perceived that it was out of envy that the chief priests had delivered him up. ¹¹ But the chief priests stirred up the crowd to have him release for them Barabbas instead. ¹² And Pilate again said to them, "Then what shall I do with the man you call the King of the Jews?" ¹³ And they cried out again, "Crucify him." ¹⁴ And Pilate said to them, "Why? What evil has he done?" But they shouted all the more, "Crucify him." ¹⁵ So Pilate, wishing to satisfy the crowd, released for them Barabbas, and having scourged[a] Jesus, he delivered him to be crucified.

15a. A Roman judicial penalty, consisting of a severe beating with a multi-lashed whip containing embedded pieces of bone and metal

Jesus Is Mocked

¹⁶ And the soldiers led him away inside the palace (that is, the governor's headquarters),[b] and they called together the whole battalion.[c] ¹⁷ And they clothed him in a purple cloak, and twisting together a crown of thorns, they put it on him. ¹⁸ And they began to salute him, "Hail, King of the Jews!" ¹⁹ And they were striking his head with a reed and spitting on him and kneeling down in homage to him. ²⁰ And when they had mocked him, they stripped him of the purple cloak and put his own clothes on him. And they led him out to crucify him.

The Crucifixion

²¹ And they compelled a passer-by, Simon of Cyrene, who was coming in from the country, the father of Alexander and Rufus, to carry his cross. ²² And they brought him to the place called Golgotha (which means Place of a Skull). ²³ And they offered him wine mixed with myrrh, but he did not take it. ²⁴ And they crucified him and divided his garments among them, casting lots for them, to decide what each should take. ²⁵ And it was the third hour[d] when they crucified him. ²⁶ And the inscription of the charge against him read, "The King of the Jews." ²⁷ And with him they crucified two robbers,

---

15b. Greek *the praetorium*
15c. Greek *cohort*; a tenth of a Roman legion, usually about 600 men
15d. That is, 9 a.m.

one on his right and one on his left.*e* 29 And those who passed by derided him, wagging their heads and saying, "Aha! You who would destroy the temple and rebuild it in three days, 30 save yourself, and come down from the cross!" 31 So also the chief priests with the scribes mocked him to one another, saying, "He saved others; he cannot save himself. 32 Let the Christ, the King of Israel, come down now from the cross that we may see and believe." Those who were crucified with him also reviled him.

The Death of Jesus

33 And when the sixth hour*f* had come, there was darkness over the whole land until the ninth hour.*g* 34 And at the ninth hour Jesus cried with a loud voice, "Eloi, Eloi, lema sabachthani?" which means, "My God, my God, why have you forsaken me?" 35 And some of the bystanders hearing it said, "Behold, he is calling Elijah." 36 And someone ran and filled a sponge with sour wine, put it on a reed and gave it to him to drink, saying, "Wait, let us see whether Elijah will come to take him down." 37 And Jesus uttered a loud cry and breathed his last. 38 And the curtain of the temple was torn in two, from top to bottom. 39 And when the centurion, who stood

---

15e. Some manuscripts insert verse 28: *And the Scripture was fulfilled that says, "He was numbered with the transgressors"*
15f. That is, noon
15g. That is, 3 p.m

facing him, saw that in this way he[h] breathed his last, he said, "Truly this man was the Son[i] of God!"

⁴⁰ There were also women looking on from a distance, among whom were Mary Magdalene, and Mary the mother of James the younger and of Joses, and Salome. ⁴¹ When he was in Galilee, they followed him and ministered to him, and there were also many other women who came up with him to Jerusalem.

Jesus Is Buried

⁴² And when evening had come, since it was the day of Preparation, that is, the day before the Sabbath, ⁴³ Joseph of Arimathea, a respected member of the Council, who was also himself looking for the kingdom of God, took courage and went to Pilate and asked for the body of Jesus. ⁴⁴ Pilate was surprised to hear that he should have already died.[j] And summoning the centurion, he asked him whether he was already dead. ⁴⁵ And when he learned from the centurion that he was dead, he granted the corpse to Joseph. ⁴⁶ And Joseph[k] bought a linen shroud, and taking him down, wrapped him in the linen shroud and laid him in a tomb that had been cut out of

---

15h. Some manuscripts insert *cried out and*
15i. Or *a son*
15j. Or *Pilate wondered whether he had already died*
15k. Greek *he*

the rock. And he rolled a stone against the entrance of the tomb. [47] Mary Magdalene and Mary the mother of Joses saw where he was laid.

The Resurrection

16 When the Sabbath was past, Mary Magdalene, Mary the mother of James, and Salome bought spices, so that they might go and anoint him. [2] And very early on the first day of the week, when the sun had risen, they went to the tomb. [3] And they were saying to one another, "Who will roll away the stone for us from the entrance of the tomb?" [4] And looking up, they saw that the stone had been rolled back – it was very large. [5] And entering the tomb, they saw a young man sitting on the right side, dressed in a white robe, and they were alarmed. [6] And he said to them, "Do not be alarmed. You seek Jesus of Nazareth, who was crucified. He has risen; he is not here. See the place where they laid him. [7] But go, tell his disciples and Peter that he is going before you to Galilee. There you will see him, just as he told you." [8] And they went out and fled from the tomb, for trembling and astonishment had seized them, and they said nothing to anyone, for they were afraid.

Jesus Appears to Mary Magdalene

[9] Now when he rose early on the first day of the week, he appeared first to Mary Magdalene, from whom he

had cast out seven demons. ¹⁰ She went and told those who had been with him, as they mourned and wept. ¹¹ But when they heard that he was alive and had been seen by her, they would not believe it.

Jesus Appears to Two Disciples

¹² After these things he appeared in another form to two of them, as they were walking into the country. ¹³ And they went back and told the rest, but they did not believe them.

The Great Commission

¹⁴ Afterwards he appeared to the eleven themselves as they were reclining at table, and he rebuked them for their unbelief and hardness of heart, because they had not believed those who saw him after he had risen. ¹⁵ And he said to them, "Go into all the world and proclaim the gospel to the whole creation. ¹⁶ Whoever believes and is baptized will be saved, but whoever does not believe will be condemned. ¹⁷ And these signs will accompany those who believe: in my name they will cast out demons; they will speak in new tongues; ¹⁸ they will pick up serpents with their hands; and if they drink any deadly poison, it will not hurt them; they will lay their hands on the sick, and they will recover."

¹⁹ So then the Lord Jesus, after he had spoken to them, was taken up into heaven and sat down at the right hand

of God. ²⁰ And they went out and preached everywhere, while the Lord worked with them and confirmed the message by accompanying signs.[a]

16a. Some of the earliest manuscripts do not include 16:9-20. Some manuscripts include after verse 8 the following: *But they reported briefly to Peter and those with him all that they had been told. And after this, Jesus himself sent out by means of them, from east to west, the sacred and imperishable proclamation of eternal salvation.* These manuscripts then continue with verses 9-20